Wayne Arthurson

First printed in 2014 10 9 8 7 6 5 4 3 2

Printed in China

The Publisher: Eschia Books Inc.

Library and Archives Canada Cataloguing in Publication

Arthurson, Wayne, 1962–, author
Spirit Animals : meanings & stories / Wayne Arthurson.

ISBN 978-1-926696-26-3 (pbk.)

1. Animals—Religious aspects. 2. Totems. 3. Indians of North America—Religion. 4. Indian mythology—North America. I. Title.

E98.R3A78 2015 299.7'1212 C2015-901359-3

Project Director: Dianne Meili
Interior Design: Gerry Dotto
Cover Image: Wolf illustration © jhamvirus / Thinkstock

Image Credits:
From Flickr: Mr.TinDC, 6; Ingrid Taylar, 7; USFWSmidwest, 11; nigel, 16; Ron Mead, 20; Franco Folini, 21; Linda Tanner, 30; Bill Damon, 70; Steve Hersey, 71; Laszlo Ilyes, 73; Olivier Bacquet, 81.

From Thinkstock: Shaun Wilkinson, 5; Herhurricane, 6; milsmilosevic, 8; Christos Georghiou, 9; Comstock, 10; igorkov, 12; VectorWerk, 10; Nick Dale, 13; mis_Tery, 14; Andrei Nikolaevich Rybachuk, 15; Purestock, 16; MikeLane45, 17; Dan Christie, 18; ksyu_deniska, 19; justinccotton photography, 20; Elena Belous, 22; Cattallina, 23; Lynn Bystrom, 24; jonmccormackphoto, 24; seread, 25; David OST, 26; EdwardVisserPhotography, 27; Glenn Nagel, 27; Kylie088, 28; magiczz, 29; David 04_McNew, 30; laski, 32; Dynamic Graphics, 33; Purestock, 34; Tom Tietz, 34, 38, 40; MikeLane45, 35; Pimonova, 36; kopirin, 37; ; RyanVincePhotography, 38; Geoff Kuchera, 39; Lonely, 41; Dymanic Graphics, 43; HIRO_amanaimagesRF, 44; Lightwriter1949, 44; gsagi, 45; eva_mask, 46; mrsopossum, 47; denisovd, 48; Ingram Publishing, 48; al_louc, 49; SkvortsovaSashas, 50, 51; mari_art, 52; MihailDechev. 53; IP, 54; DeDron, 55; JohnPitcher, 56; Richard Wear_Design Pics, 56; AndreAnita, 57; seamartini, 58; insima, 59, 94; Design Pics, 60; Jupiterimages, 60; kelly lovesphotography, 61; KsanasK, 62; Esdelval, 63; Gkuchera, 64; Smirnov Vasily, 64; John Pitcher, 65; Leon Belomlinsky, 66; vectorcartoons, 67; Ka Ho Leung, 68; FX Kushartono, 69; Dean_Fikar, 70; Dorling Kindersley, 72; latsalomao, 74; Juha Remes, 74; Michael Fitzsimmons, 75; Tribalium. 76, 95; James Arrington, 77; Brian Lasenby, 78; porojnicu, 78; Dawn Hudson, 80; Evgeniya Lazareva, 83; Alexey Burmakin, 84;Perry Albrigo, 85; DanBachKristnesen, 86; Murphy_Shewchuk, 86; Fuse, 87; LeshaBu, 88; LeshaBu, 89; crash1965, 90; MikeLane45, 90; Yan Gluzberg, 91; PaulReevesPhotography, 92; Ka Ho Leung, 93.

From Wikipedia: MONGO, 31; D Gordon E Robertson, 79; public domain, 82; Robert Pittman_NOAA, 82.

Produced with the assistance of the Government of Alberta, Alberta Media Fund.

Alberta Government

PC: 28

Contents

Introduction

Animals were important to North America's First People. They relied on animals for food, clothing, shelter, tools, weapons, medicines, ceremonies, jewelry and for many other purposes. They used every part of the animal. Wasting or throwing away parts of the animal was thought to be bad behavior.

Some people saw animals as lesser creatures. Native people saw animals and humans as part of the whole world, each no better than the other. They did hunt animals. But many Native cultures believed that the animals sacrificed themselves so humans could survive. Wasting parts of the animal dishonored that sacrifice.

Aboriginal people believed all animals had spirits. When an animal died or was killed, its spirit lived on. Sometimes it returned to where the animal had lived on the earth. For example, the salmon would return to the ocean to become another salmon. Other times, the animal spirit moved to a different kind of existence. If the animal was killed and its body was not treated with respect, the spirit of the animal could stay behind and cause trouble. To respect the animal's sacrifice, Native peoples performed certain rituals to satisfy the animal's spirit.

Native people believed animals had spirits and could gift individuals with healing and offer guidance. They paid attention to their behavior and gave them descriptions. They used these in stories and ceremonies and passed them down from generation to generation. The descriptions became an important part of their lives and their culture.

Our ancestors did not create the descriptions of animals from nothing. For thousands of years, they watched animals. They used what they saw to develop the folklore and attitudes toward animals and their spirits. From nature and the environment they shaped their culture.

About This Book

This book should only be seen as a guide. It is meant to introduce the importance of animals to Native people. You may see if the meanings behind these animal spirits are reflected in your own life. Just remember that Native cultures were diverse. Each one had its own ideas about the world, including animals. To some cultures some animals were more important than to others.

You the reader may make a connection with a certain spirit animal. It may be through your birthday, if you are a member of that animal clan or for some other reason. You should remember that the animal spirit is not to be worshiped the way some other cultures might worship a god. You are meant to follow a spirit animal. You can ask for guidance or help, but you should speak in the same way as you might to a guardian angel.

Even though you may follow a particular spirit animal, that doesn't mean you can't connect to another animal. Have an open mind when reading about these animal spirits and know there are different meanings to learn from each one.

Crow

Crows are smart. They are tricksters, intelligent but keen to have fun tricking people and other animals. This is not seen as a bad thing. Some of the most important spirit animals are tricksters. They are the cultural heroes of many nations in North America.

Crows began in Central Asia then moved into North America and the rest of the world. They are adaptable creatures that eat a wide variety of foods, including insects, smaller birds, fish, fruit and vegetables and carrion (dead animals). Crows can be trained to count, use tools, recognize themselves in mirrors and tell humans apart by their facial features. They are observant and learn by watching and predicting what will happen next.

The crow's intelligence and observation skills are important in stories about crows and what they mean. They may also be why Native people view the bird as a trickster. If you come across a crow or feel the need to follow one, there may be a major shift happening in your life. Be willing and ready to accept the change. The change can be good or it may be a difficult adjustment. You may need to take action. If you adapt, you will survive and push through the difficult time.

The appearance of a crow in your life, maybe in a dream, may also mean that you are about to be tricked or fooled. Be on your guard. Or perhaps you are getting signs from other spirits, but you haven't been able to figure out the meaning of these signs. The crow's appearance in your life may help you discover the truth.

The Rainbow Crow (Lenape)

Before the Lenape lived on the earth, the weather was warm and the animals were happy. One day, snow covered the earth, and the world became cold. The animals became worried. They decided to send someone to Kishelamàkänk, the Creator, to ask him to stop the snow.

"I will go," said a voice from above. It was the rainbow crow, the brightest and most colorful bird of all. The rainbow crow was smart and could sing beautiful songs in a lovely voice. The perfect choice!

The rainbow crow flew high above the earth for three days, past the winds and the clouds, past the moon and the stars to the home of the Creator. But the Creator was too busy to notice him.

The crow sang a beautiful song.

"What a wonderful gift of song," the Creator said, finally. "In return, I will give you what you want."

The rainbow crow asked the Creator to stop the snow.

"I cannot," replied the Creator. "The snow has a spirit of its own."

"Then please will you make it warm again," pleaded the rainbow crow.

"One day I will. But not for many months."

"How will the animals stay warm?" the rainbow crow asked.

"All I can do is give you this." The Creator picked up a long stick and poked it into the sun. The stick caught fire and gave off great heat.

"Fire will keep you warm. But I will give you this only once. Hurry back to earth before the flame goes out."

The rainbow crow flew back to earth carrying the fire on the stick. On the first day, sparks from the fire burned the crow's tail feathers. On the second day, the soot from the flame turned the rainbow crow's feathers black. On the third day, the smoke and ash blew into the crow's mouth, so the crow could only make a "caw-caw" sound. The crow reached the earth. The heat from the fire melted the snow, warming the other animals.

And so the world received fire. Everyone gave thanks to the rainbow crow. But the crow's feathers had turned black, and he could no longer sing. The crow was sad and began to cry.

The Creator heard the crying and told the crow not to worry.

"Soon, man will come to the earth. He will become the master of all, except you. Man will never hurt you because your meat tastes like fire and smoke. He will never capture you because you no longer have a beautiful voice. Your feathers will have no value because they are black. But in the black of your feathers, all the colors will be seen. The crow will always be free."

Eagle

Almost every Native group honors the eagle. Many peoples consider the eagle the chief of the birds because of its hunting skill and its courage to fly higher than all other birds. They believe the Creator lives high in the sky and sees all from above. Eagles fly closest to the Creator, so they are thought to be deeply connected to the Great Spirit.

Species of eagles are found on every continent except Antarctica. There are four basic groups: fish eagles, booted eagles, snake eagles and giant forest eagles. The most common and well-known eagles in North America are the bald eagle of the fish group and the golden eagle, a booted eagle.

Eagles soar above the world, looking down and seeing hidden truths and the overall pattern of the world. Eagles are strong fliers with keen eyesight. They have graceful strength and power balanced with intuition. Their animal spirit is connected with esteemed leaders and teachers, and with the qualities of strength and courage. People who connect with the eagle spirit may show signs of this majestic bird's power. But you must respect the eagle's power and not be prideful. Nor should you look down on others if they follow other spirit animals. To behave in this way is not in the eagle's nature.

The eagle feather is one of the most prized totems in many Native communities. Finding an eagle feather is considered a sacred event in someone's life. It is a sign of great fortune or a sign that the finder has been blessed. If the finder then gives the feather to someone else, they are showing respect

and honor for that person. In some cultures, it is customary for a person to give a feather to an elder they admire or to a person who has done great things.

Because eagles are known to be excellent hunters, many Plains people gave eagle feathers to warriors who were courageous in battle. Even today, some Native peoples offer eagle feathers to individuals who have shown greatness.

In the United States, it is illegal to sell eagle feathers or to kill an eagle to get its feathers.

The Eagle and the Linnet (origin unknown)

A long time ago, all the birds argued about which one was the best flier.

"I'm the fastest flier," said the hummingbird. He dashed about, back and forth among all the other birds.

"No, I'm the best," said the duck. "Every fall I fly for weeks at a time to get away from winter."

"Ha," said the Owl. "None of you can fly in the dark like me."

"We should have a race," said the linnet, a small dull bird that lived in the bushes. "The bird that flies the highest in the sky will be named the best flier."

Even though the linnet was a bit of trickster, the birds agreed to have the contest the next day.

When all the birds gathered for the start of the race, the linnet was missing. But everyone was so excited they didn't notice. Some flew fast but dropped away, some were strong but they became tired. After a while, only the eagle, with its long, strong wings, was left. It seemed to touch the sky.

Before the eagle could claim victory, the linnet appeared. The small bird had hitched a ride on the back of the eagle and was flying slightly higher.

"I flew the highest," the linnet said. "So I am the best flier."

The other birds did not agree. The eagle had flown the highest and showed bravery by almost touching the sky. And since he had to carry another bird on his back, the eagle was deemed the strongest of the birds. So all the birds honored the eagle.

To this day, bravery and strength are honored with the gift of an eagle feather.

Owl

Owls are mysterious creatures sometimes thought to be an omen of death. But death is just another part of life, so the owl is not considered evil by many Native cultures. It is simply unknowable because it is a night creature. To many peoples, death does not always mean the end of life. It may just mean the end of one part of a life and the beginning of another, such as moving from elementary school to junior high.

Of the more than 200 species of owls almost all are nocturnal. They have a keen sense of sight and hearing, and the ability to turn their heads almost completely around. Owls have large eyes compared to the size of their bodies. They are birds of prey that hunt other animals. Their ears and eyes are at the front of their heads, rather than at the side like other birds.

Owls rely on stealth and surprise to capture their prey. Most have a dull color that makes them almost invisible. Owls also have notches on the feathers at the edges of their wings, allowing them to flap their wings quietly. Because owls can see and hunt silently and successfully in darkness where humans cannot, many Native cultures see them as dark animals with a mysterious power to be respected.

Some clans, mostly in the southern U.S., follow the owl. Owl carvings also appear on totem poles in the Pacific Northwest.

People who seek or follow the owl are not evil. They tend to be interested in the unknown and the mysterious. They like to explore the different levels of existence. One can gain wisdom by following the owl. The owl can see in the dark, so some believe that those who follow or encounter the owl are looking for guidance for the future. The owl may also help discover hidden talents or skills in yourself and others. Many who follow the owl are artists, writers, teachers or conservationists.

Why the Owl Has Big Eyes (Iroquois)

A long time ago when the world was being made, Raweno, the Everything Maker, was busy creating all the animals, plants, rocks, forest, lakes, rivers, mountains and all the things that cover the earth.

Raweno had started creating the owl but was not finished. The owl was impatient, so as Raweno was working, the owl kept talking.

"I want a long neck like the swan," Owl demanded. "And red feathers like the cardinal and a beak like the hawk."

"You must wait your turn," said Raweno. "I am creating the rabbit."

"Can I have long legs and ears? And fangs? And sharp claws?" asked the rabbit.

"Yes, we can give you some claws and fangs," said the Everything Maker, patting the rabbit's new long ears.

"Silly Rabbit. You should ask for wisdom. That's something you can really use," shouted the owl.

"Wait your turn, Owl!" shouted Raweno.

"I demand wisdom," shouted the owl.

"You were warned, Owl!" shouted Raweno. He pushed the owl's head down into his body, making the owl's neck disappear. He then shook the bird roughly, making the owl's eyes widen in fright. He pulled on the owl's ears until they stuck out from his head.

Raweno snapped his fingers. "There you go, Owl. Now you can listen better, see better and turn your head more. You also have wisdom. Now use that wisdom to fly away before I take everything away."

Since the owl now had wisdom, it flew away quickly. Raweno turned around to give the rabbit fangs and claws, but the rabbit had run away, frightened.

Raven

The raven is fascinating. Because of its dark color, it is connected to darkness and the night. The bird also evokes themes of creation, the trickster spirit and selfishness because of its intelligence and survival skills.

It is the intelligence of ravens, compared to other birds, that is reflected in Aboriginal spirituality and stories. Many Native cultures don't recognize the difference between the crow and the raven in their stories. However, ravens are much bigger than crows and mostly prefer to live in wilderness areas. Ravens can also make over 30 different types of sounds that crows cannot make. They can also fly higher than crows so are found in more places than crows.

However, both the raven and the crow are signs of good fortune because they have no natural predators.

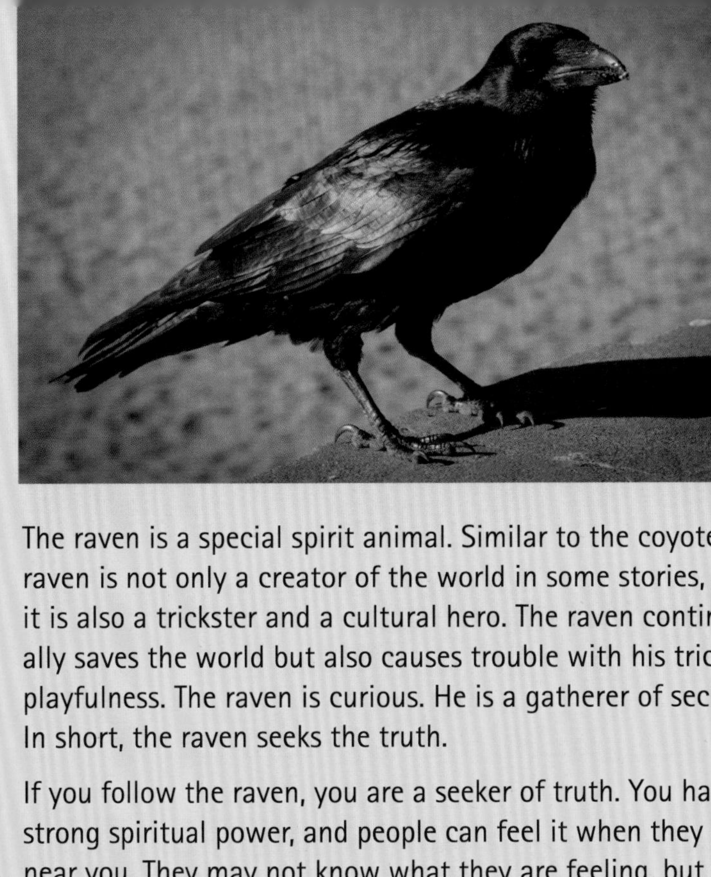

The raven is a special spirit animal. Similar to the coyote, the raven is not only a creator of the world in some stories, but it is also a trickster and a cultural hero. The raven continually saves the world but also causes trouble with his trickster playfulness. The raven is curious. He is a gatherer of secrets. In short, the raven seeks the truth.

If you follow the raven, you are a seeker of truth. You have strong spiritual power, and people can feel it when they are near you. They may not know what they are feeling, but they know it's coming from you. You also have the ability to respond quickly and are decisive when the need arises. The raven likes shiny objects and other animals but also seeks solitude.

If you encounter a raven, something magical may happen to you. Pay attention to your dreams in case they give clues for the near future. You may notice coincidences a few days after the dream. These coincidences may or may not have meaning, so don't try too hard to figure them out. Just be aware of their presence. Of course, because a raven is a playful trickster, the appearance of the bird could also mean nothing.

The Raven and the Seagull (Tlingit)

When the world was created, the Great Spirit gave boxes to the animals that lived in the world before humans. Inside the boxes were mountains, fire, water, wind, seeds, oceans and trees, everything the world needed to flourish.

When the animals opened their boxes, these items were released into the world. The animals were excited, but something was missing. There was no sun, no moon and no stars in the world. None of the animals could see in the darkness.

The animals looked to see who had the box containing light. It was the seagull. The seagull was greedy. It refused to open the box, holding it tightly under its wing.

"Please open your box," the animals pleaded with the seagull. "Open your box so we can have light."

"No, I won't," the seagull cried. "It's my box, all mine. I'm never going to open it."

"Please seagull, don't be greedy," begged the animals. "Open your box, and share the light with the world."

"No it's mine," the seagull replied. "I'm never going to share it with you."

The raven, because it was smart and could sometimes trick others into doing things they didn't want to do, tried to persuade the seagull.

The seagull knew the raven would try to talk him into opening his box so he held on tighter. "I'm not going to listen to you, Raven. You may be a trickster, but nothing you say can make me open my box and share it with the world.

But the raven said nothing. It walked up to the seagull, picked up a thorn and stuck it into the seagull's foot. The seagull yelled in pain but didn't open the box.

Finally, the raven pushed the thorn in deeper until the pain caused the seagull to drop the box. The raven grabbed the box and opened it. Out of the box came the sun, moon and stars, bringing light to the world. And so the first day began.

Bear

Bears are large, powerful animals. The spirit associated with them is strength. Bears are featured in Aboriginal mythology because the animal is a major being, both physically and spiritually. People respect bears and tell many stories about them.

Bears are at the top of the food chain. They have no predators except for humans. They are great hunters, able to fell a moose or grab salmon from a rushing river. Bears are also omnivores, meaning they eat all types of food, including insects, honey and berries.

Also known as protectors, the bear is a symbol of leadership and wisdom. The bear is called "Grandfather" and given the respect of an honored elder. The people of the Haida Gwaii in the Pacific Northwest call the bear "Elder Kinsmen." When a Haida kills a bear, eagle down is sprinkled on the bear's body to show respect. Conversely, in many stories, bears are also seen as bumbling, silly animals.

If you follow the bear, you see yourself as confident with a commanding presence. When a bear walks into a room, people pay attention. But be careful about being over-confident. Bears are confident, but they shouldn't use that confidence to overpower others. Be ready to listen to others.

Bears hibernate during the winter, and if the bear is your spirit animal, you may learn things more easily or be more creative when you are alone. Bears represent wisdom, healing, protection and insight. Meeting a bear, either physically, in a dream or during a spirit quest, tells you that you are near a sacred place, and that your presence has been noted and is being studied.

That said, you should never go on any quest, physically or otherwise, searching for bears because these animals are temperamental. Their territory must be respected, and if a bear comes to you, respect it.

Bears are strong medicine. In some tribes, it is disrespectful, even dangerous, to insult bears. You must avoid stepping on bear scat and must not mention the animal's name outside of certain sacred ceremonies.

Muin and the Medicine (Mik'maq)

In the beginning of time, the people lived in harmony with the land, the plants and the animals. The people knew all their brothers and sisters were there to help them live, so they sang songs to celebrate. One spring day Muin, the bear, was in the forest, and he heard the songs. The people were singing a song asking him to help them find the medicines to help them thrive.

Muin knew he would have to make a journey to the spirit world in order to help the people. During the spring and summer, Muin ate all that he could because he knew his journey would be a long one. In late fall, he looked for a lodge so his body would be safe while he was on his journey. Just before winter arrived, he went into the lodge and fell into a deep sleep.

While his body slept, his spirit traveled into the spirit world. Muin asked the council of the plant people for some of their medicines. The plant people agreed but told Muin that he

first must promise to cultivate and fertilize the land for them so they could come back every year. Muin accepted their offer and asked the other animals to do the same. The plant people shared their medicines with him.

Finally, Muin realized his journey was over. When he returned he met a woman called Miumiskw, the Bear Woman. He told her which berries she should pick and the order in which they should be picked every year. He told her which fish should be caught and how they should be caught. He told her which animals the people should hunt and how they should be hunted and used.

To this day, Muin tills and fertilizes. He digs for food and berries, and the plants continue to grow. In the winter, he returns to his lodge so he can again make the journey to the spirit world.

Buffalo

To Native Peoples of the Great Plains of North America, the buffalo, also called American Bison, was the most important animal. Before the Europeans arrived, over 50 million buffalo lived on the Great Plains. The animals were vital to the ecosystem as a major source of food for animals and humans.

Buffalo hunting was a traditional part of life for the Great Plains people such as the Cree, Cherokee, Blackfoot and others. But it was not easy. The average male buffalo can weigh almost a ton and run twice as fast as the fastest human. Hunting the animal was dangerous, and before the 1500s,

Native people did not have horses. The most spectacular way that they hunted buffalo long ago was by using a buffalo jump. A group of people, often an entire community or collection of communities, chased a herd of buffalo over several miles. The animals soon formed a stampede. The people herded the buffalo toward a high cliff, a buffalo jump. The buffalo would fall over the cliff to their deaths.

Because the buffalo was key to the survival of many peoples, it is an important spirit animal. It is a positive influence, connected with endurance, strength and protection. Those who follow the buffalo are generous and always try to see the good in people. If you meet a buffalo in a dream or on a spiritual journey, it may be a sign telling you not to feel sorry for yourself. You have many strengths and resources within you to call upon.

One of the most sacred animals is the white buffalo. If you encounter this animal in a dream, it is strong medicine. The appearance of a white buffalo could mean a miracle or another important event in your life.

How the Buffalo Hunt Began (Cheyenne)

In the early days of the world, the buffalo hunted humans. The magpie and the hawk were on the side of the people because neither hunted the other. One day, a race was held between the animals and humans. The winners would be allowed to eat the losers.

The racecourse covered a long distance around a vast mountain. One of the swiftest animals to enter the race was a buffalo named Neika, meaning Swift Head. The magpie and the hawk offered to race for the humans.

The birds and other animals painted themselves for the race, and since that time, they have been brightly colored. The water turtle put red paint around his eyes, and the dark-colored magpie painted his belly and shoulders white. At last, all the animals were ready for the race. They stood in a row at the start line.

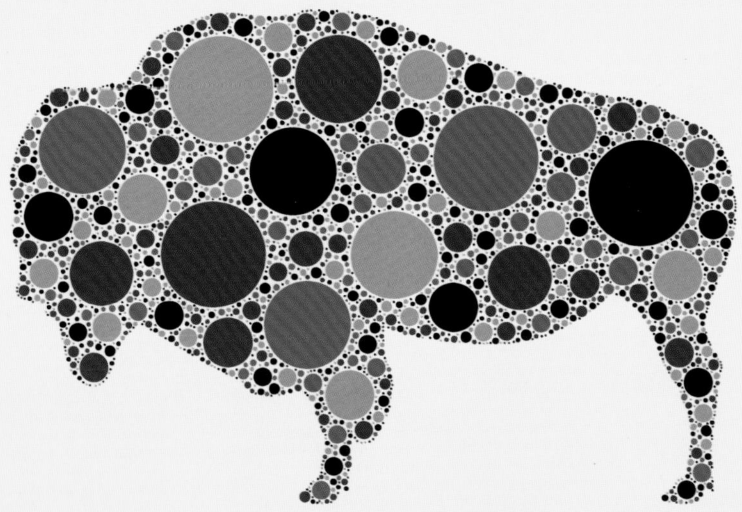

Once the race started, the animals ran and ran. They made loud noises instead of singing to inspire them to run faster. But all the small birds and animals such as coyotes, flies, ants and snakes were left behind. Neika was in the lead, followed by the magpie, the hawk and then the people. All around the mountain, Neika led the race, but the magpie and hawk knew they could win and kept up with Neika until they neared the finish line. Both birds swooped past the buffalo and won the race for the people.

Because the two birds had won the race for the people, the buffalo told their young to hide from the people who were now going to hunt them. From that day on, the Cheyenne began to hunt buffalo. Since the magpie and the hawk had won the race for the people, they do not eat these birds. They use the birds' beautiful feathers as ornaments or wear them on their clothing.

Cougar

The cougar, also called puma or mountain lion, is the largest cat in North America. It is one of nature's greatest hunters, easily bringing down a deer or other large animal. The cougar's ability to hunt silently resonated with Aboriginal societies. Many Native groups used the model of the cougar's patience and silent hunting to teach young warriors hunting skills.

Cougars are long, lean animals. At over 200 pounds (90 kilos), the male cougar is larger than the female. They hunt over a wide area for their prey, including deer, goats, rabbits and mice.

Because cougars move silently, they can move easily between the physical and spiritual worlds. People who have the cougar as their spirit animal move quietly and stealthily through life, seemingly unnoticed. They always have a goal in mind. When the goal is in sight, they act quickly without delay to achieve their goal. But their actions may surprise others.

Cougars also signify balance and grace with wildness. They prefer to spend time alone but also enjoy being with family.

If you encounter a cougar in any way, it is a rare event. Be respectful. The wildness of the animal is strong medicine. The cougar doesn't like to be seen, so any view or vision of a cougar animal spirit will be short. Like the bear, do not go looking for cougars. The sight of a cougar, in your dreams or in real life, tells you that it's time to make a decision about something you are putting off. Be clear and open to others about what you want. Move slowly without anyone noticing until it is time to act, or you may lose what you seek. Seeing a cougar may also mean it is time to get balance and grace in your life.

The Cougar, the Wolf, the Fox and the Bobcat (Shoshone)

A long time ago, the Shoshone lived in harmony in a forested area with many rivers. They had plenty of water and food.

One day, a vicious group of little warrior people attacked the Shoshone. The warriors were experts with the bow and arrow. They drove the Shoshone out of their lands.

The Shoshone sent their medicine man on a vision quest to find out how to get rid of the little warrior people. The old medicine man headed into the forest, following a bright star that led him into a clearing.

In the middle of the clearing he saw the wolf, the fox, the bobcat and the cougar. The cougar had a head of a man, and its paws resembled human hands. The old medicine man was scared because he had never seen anything like it before.

"Do not be afraid," said the cougar. "We are all spirits here to help you."

The medicine man asked if the cougar and the other spirits could help get rid of the mean people.

"We will help, but the Shoshone must promise to never hunt the cougar, the fox, the wolf and the bobcat."

Because the cougar was a powerful animal, the medicine man agreed.

The spirits began singing their prayers. The old medicine man flew into the air. Lightning shot down from the sky, lighting the forest on fire and killing all the vicious little people. When the fire went out, the medicine man returned to the ground.

"We have helped you," said the cougar, "so you must keep your promise."

And the Shoshone never again hunted the cougar, the bobcat, the wolf or the fox.

Coyote

The coyote is a major figure for many North American Native cultures. In the stories, the coyote is seen as hero, villain, clown, Creator and trickster, often all of these characters combined.

Coyotes are popular because they live in almost every area of North America, even on the tundra and in major cities. They are smart, adaptable animals that live in family packs. Coyotes are great hunters, but they can also eat almost anything, including carrion and garbage.

Coyotes are many things to Native cultures, especially tricksters who play jokes on other animals and humans. Or the coyote may get into trouble but survives because of its cunning. Coyotes can also be villains, heroes, jokesters, even the Creator of the world. But its main role is the trickster character.

Tricksters are neither good nor bad, neither stupid nor overly smart. In many ways, they are similar to humans. Another reason for the coyote's popularity has to do with the Aboriginal concept of humor. Laughter relaxes the mind and body, allowing one to become closer to the world. The trickster role of coyote shows that surprise and fun are an important part of being alive.

The coyote always tries to find the humorous side of a situation because laughter is the best medicine. Those who follow the coyote as a spirit animal do the same. That doesn't mean they are always clowns, but they never take themselves too seriously.

The coyote is also a talented teacher and leads by example. They are often the one everyone turns to for advice, leadership or knowledge.

Coyotes are resourceful and react quickly to new situations. Nothing throws off a coyote.

If you encounter a coyote, it is strong medicine. What the coyote may tell you, either through actions or words, may not make sense, but there is strong medicine at work. You will not get easy answers. He might even try to trick you. Listen and watch carefully, and look deep inside yourself to pick up the message. Never dismiss the coyote even if you cannot understand him.

Coyote and the Monster (Nez Perce)

A long time ago, no people lived on the earth. Only animals. One day a monster came and ate everything. Only the coyote survived because he was quick and cunning. The monster could never catch him.

Coyote was angry at the monster for eating all his friends and family. So Coyote climbed the tallest mountain and tied himself with rope to the top of a tree to entice the monster. When Coyote saw the monster walk by in the valley, Coyote yelled at the monster.

"Come eat me, you silly monster!" Coyote said. "I am the last animal alive."

The monster was big but could not reach the mountaintop. Every time it tried to climb, its weight pulled it down. The monster even tried to blow Coyote off the mountain. The wind was stronger than the strongest blizzard but could not blow Coyote off the mountain.

The monster realized that Coyote was clever, so he made a new plan. Instead of being angry at Coyote, the monster invited Coyote to his lodge.

Coyote agreed to go to the monster's lodge, but only if he could visit all his friends.

"I ate all of your friends," said the monster with a contented smile. "They are in my stomach."

"Can I visit them to see if you are treating them right?" asked Coyote. "That way I will know if you are a good creature, and I can visit with you."

That's an even better plan, thought the monster. *I will eat Coyote when he visits his friends.*

So the monster opened its mouth wide, and Coyote slid into the monster's stomach.

Coyote's friends were sleeping because the monster had eaten them. But Coyote had a plan. Using his teeth and claws, Coyote cut the monster's stomach open, killing it. All of the animals woke up and escaped. They thanked Coyote for saving them.

Coyote broke apart the dead monster to create a new animal so it wouldn't rise again to eat all of the animals. He threw the many pieces to the four directions, north, south, east and west. Wherever a piece of the monster landed, people were created.

Deer

Deer have always been a key source of food for many Native peoples of North America. Deer hide was also used for clothing, footwear and material for dwellings. Hides were also used for making instruments, such as the drums used in sacred ceremonies. The antlers of the deer, mostly of the males, were used to make tools or weapons. Deer, like many other hunted animals, sacrificed themselves to feed humans. They deserved respect and honor. Many cultures performed rituals of thanks when a deer was killed.

The people had other uses for deer other than just as a source of food. The diet of the deer was a guide to show them which berries and plants were not poisonous. Because of this, the deer was seen as a teacher, a guardian of the humans and a guide for survival in the natural world. To some, deer may seem weak because they are easily hunted. However, deer can adjust to changes in the environment more easily than most predators. Deer can also blend with their surroundings and can move away quickly.

If you follow the deer as a spirit animal, you have deep connection to nature, full of grace, but with strength. A deer is a keen observer but doesn't attract attention.

If a deer comes close to your fire, it wishes to deliver a message from the spirit world. Ask it to come to you in a dream and speak to you there. It may offer wise advice. If you follow the deer, you should also pay attention to your intuition. You are the best judge in deciding how to react to any challenges.

Meesink and the Creator (Lenape)

Long ago, the Creator was working on building the world. The animals thought creating humans was a bad idea. They spoke to Meesink, a powerful spirit.

"Meesink," said the animals. "Please ask the Creator not to create humans?"

Meesink thought the animals had a point. He went to visit the Creator in his lodge.

"Creator, we love your creation of the world. It is a wonderful place," said Meesink. "But we think creating humans is not a good idea. They will hunt all the animals. They will dig in the earth and chop down the trees. They will fill the rivers and lakes with poison and make the air stink.

The Creator nodded. "I understand what you are saying, but I have a deeper knowledge than you of what I am doing. Still, we will have a contest to decide who is right. Can you see that mountain there?"

Meesink could see a huge mountain out the window. He nodded.

"Whoever is able to move the mountain the most will decide if I should continue making humans," said the Creator.

Meesink went up to the mountain and pushed as hard as he could, using all his magic. He could not move the mountain.

Just as the Creator was about to take his turn, Meesink heard a sound. He turned to see what it was, and his face hit the mountain. He knew he had just heard a deer rushing by.

Meesink realized that the humans would be fine as long as they had the deer. They would use it for their food, their clothing and their tools.

"I see that there must be deer for the humans," said Meesink. "Please put me in charge of the woodlands where the deer live. I will make sure that humans always have the deer."

To this day, Meesink has kept his promise. He has taken care of the deer. Many great animals have existed on this world, and many are gone. The deer are still here.

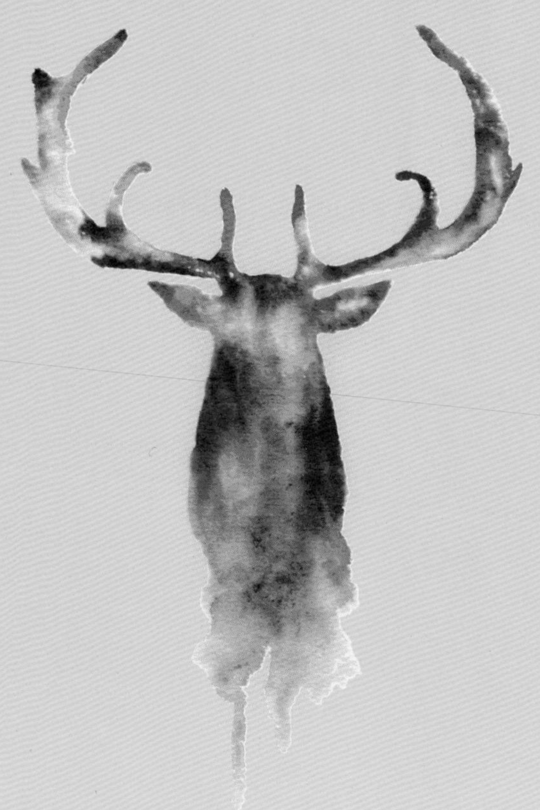

Dog

Dogs were loyal companions to many Indigenous peoples of North America. They aided in hunting, tracking and killing prey. They were useful as pack animals, especially for the Plains and Inuit cultures. For the Inuit of the High Arctic, dogs were key to survival in harsh conditions.

All dogs, regardless of breed, are descended from wolves that began living close to and interacting with humans. Both humans and dogs benefited from living together. Dogs who lived with humans had a more regular food supply. They were safer because humans were taller and able to see predators at a distance. Although humans used dogs for many purposes, even food at times, these animals had a better chance of breeding successfully than wild dogs. Their litters also had a better chance of survival because humans cared for them.

Scientists have noted that the taming and use of dogs by humans was one of the most important events in human history. It is a key reason humans became successful as a species.

Dogs are loyal friends and helpers to humans. Loyalty plays a major role for those who belong to the dog clan or who follow dogs as a spirit animal. These people are intelligent and faithful and look for the same traits in friends and partners. Dogs are known for working for humanity. Those who follow the dog, enjoy work that benefits humanity.

If you follow the dog as your spirit animal, you may feel protected or watched over. Dogs are faithful guides in exploring the spirit world. They can warn explorers of dark threats.

If you encounter a dog, either in a dream or meditation, it may mean you are lonely and need companionship. If you are having trouble with a task or relationship, the dog will guide you through your problems. Seeing the dog is a sign that you should donate some of your time and effort to help others and that you should be loyal to the important people in your life. The dog truly is humanity's best friend.

Where Dogs Came From (Plains Cree)

Long ago, there lived a hunter, his wife and their only child. The winter that year was bitterly cold. Deep snow covered the ground, and hunting was difficult. One day the hunter found the tracks of a buffalo and followed them for a long time. But it was too cold, and the snow was too deep for him to go far. When he returned home, he stood outside his tipi, scraping the snow from his moccasins. Inside, he could hear his wife talking to their crying and hungry son.

"Don't cry, my son," said the mother. "Perhaps your father has killed a buffalo. That's why he is late."

Hearing those words, the hunter knew he could not go inside empty-handed. He walked back into the cold night to continue hunting. It was a cold night, but just before dawn he came upon more buffalo tracks and followed them. He thought of his hungry family and kept going, but then he became tired and started crying, thinking he would never catch up to the buffalo.

Suddenly a wolf ran up to him. "Why are you weeping?" it asked.

"My wife and child are starving," he told the wolf. "I need to catch this buffalo."

"I will help you," said the wolf. "Hide behind these bushes, and I will drive the buffalo to you. We will share whatever you get."

When he heard the buffalo coming toward him, he took up his bow and shot six buffalo. The wolf returned soon after.

"What luck did you have?" it asked the man.

"I got six," said the man.

The wolf took some meat for his family, and the man took some for his. That night they all ate until they were full. Later, they moved their camp to where he'd stored the rest of the meat. From then on, the wolves remained with the hunter's family, helped them hunt and became their faithful their companions.

Horse

One of the most common images of Native peoples is of painted warriors astride beautiful horses. The connection between Aboriginal peoples and the horse seems timeless. But horses are not native to North America. The Europeans brought them, so most Native cultures weren't introduced to horses until the mid-1500s or later.

For many cultures, especially those who lived on the Great Plains, the horse quickly became a mainstay of their lifestyle. In less than a generation, horses became a key form of transportation, allowing farther and faster travel. This capability led many Native peoples to encounter unfamiliar tribes.

The contact had both good and bad results. More contact increased trade and alliances. But soon alliances were turned against others who weren't part of the alliance. Having horses also meant that warriors could strike enemies more quickly and from a greater distance.

Hunting was also dramatically different on the horse. No longer did hunters have to travel great distances on foot in search of buffalo and other game. They did not have to wait for the buffalo. They could go to the buffalo.

If you follow the horse as a spirit animal, you have endurance and strength to take long journeys, physical or spiritual. The horse can boost energy, especially if you need to travel but feel tired.

The horse is a powerful spirit animal, symbolizing freedom and the spirit of the wind. It also has a messenger image. The horse is a sacred animal with powerful medicine.

Wind Horse (origin unknown)

A long time ago an animal called Wind Horse was the fastest of all the ponies. It felt no fear because no one wanted to harm him. If one of the people was injured, Wind Horse cared for the person and let them ride on his back.

One day, Wind Horse was running when he heard a cry. He ran to the edge of a forest, and he found a boy whose leg was caught in a bear trap.

The boy could not move, so Wind Horse let him get on his back. When the boy rode Wind Horse, a new sense of freedom filled his heart. It was what Wind Horse always felt. The boy understood at last what it felt like to have a family.

Wind Horse knew that the boy would not heal. So the horse took the boy to the hunting grounds for those who no longer lived in the real world. At the hunting grounds, the boy would be made whole and never again feel fear, pain, hate or need.

As they rode on, Wind Horse began to love the boy. As they approached the hunting grounds, something changed in the horse. While he worried he would no longer be free to run

where he pleased by himself, Wind Horse knew it was even better to be with someone he loved.

When he saw the size of the hunting grounds, he knew there would be plenty of new and different places for him to run. Now he had someone to share it with him.

Wind Horse and the boy crossed over into the hunting grounds. Wind Horse knew that he would never return to the real world. He worried that the people would forget that he and his kind ever existed. Before he crossed over with the boy, he asked the Creator to send a reminder to the people of the friendship between Wind Horse and the boy.

A long time later, the horse was sent to the people. It had been so long that they had forgotten these animals had ever existed. But once they climbed on the horse's back, they remembered. They remembered what the boy felt when he rode Wind Horse for the first time. The feeling of riding a horse was like being with one's family.

Polar Bear

Because polar bears are animals of the High Arctic, only the Inuit, and the Dene, share the same habitat with this bear, one of the largest land carnivores (meat-eating animals) on Earth.

One of the similarities all Inuit groups have is their respect for the polar bear. The Inuit of Labrador believe that the polar bear is the embodiment of a great spirit because it is a great hunter. There aren't many plants in the High Arctic so polar bears are true carnivores. They are also one of the few true apex predators (a predator with no predator of its own), except men. Polar bears are highly respected and should be given much distance when encountered.

Polar bears weigh up to 1750 pounds (795 kilos), perfectly suited for life in the Arctic. White fur allows the animal to blend in with the environment. The skin under its fur is black, which absorbs heat and helps keep the polar bear warm. The

follicles of its fur are hollow, trapping warm air and helping the polar bear swim more easily. Their fur is also a bit greasy and their feet are webbed, so they are comfortable in the water and on land.

The Inuit learned to hunt seals by watching polar bears. Seals make breathing holes in the ice, coming to one when they need to breath. Polar bears and humans stand at these breathing holes, waiting for a seal to pop up.

The Inuit see spirit animals differently. They believe that all animals, like humans, have souls or spirits, and that the soul lives on after the animal has died. If a hunter kills a polar bear, he must honor its spirit or it could seek revenge on him and his family.

Because the Inuit hunt seal the same way that polar bears do, the bear is respected as a teacher. It symbolizes strength, physical confidence and the ability to adapt to any situation. Polar bears should never be taken for granted or thought of casually. Heed the polar bear. Its animal spirit commands respect.

Having a polar bear spirit means you are assertive in your communications and actions. Pause and observe what is going on around you, and when the time is right, act with focus and do not hesitate. Only complete the task at hand rather than focusing on unimportant matters.

Why the Stars Are in the Sky (Inuit)

To the Inuit, stars are living beings, sent to roam the sky forever. One of the stars is known as Nanuk, the spirit of the bear.

One day Nanuk was hunting. He spent many hours at a seal hole with no luck. So he kept looking around for something to eat. But Nanuk was also being hunted. A group of Inuit had spotted him by the seal hole, but he did not see them. After stalking him for a while, they set a pack of six dogs on him. Nanuk could fight a few dogs off, but not all six. So Nanuk ran away. He ran a long way over the ice, trying to get away from the dogs.

Nanuk tried to find some open water, but it was the middle of winter so much of the water was frozen over. Nanuk ran faster, but the dogs still chased after him. They ran for hours and hours, Nanuk trying hard to get away, and the dogs trying hard to catch him.

In the excitement of the hunt, Nanuk and the dogs did not realize how close to the edge of the world they were getting. When they reached the edge, they kept on going, jumping directly into the sky where they became stars. To this day, Nanuk is forever pursued in the sky by that same pack of dogs.

The constellation that makes up Nanuk and the hunting dogs is one of the most prominent constellations in the winter sky. It is one of the first to appear in the winter. It is almost directly overhead by the middle of the winter night, but lying partly in the southern part of the sky. The Europeans called the constellation Pleiades, also known as the Seven Sisters for its seven brightest stars. To the Inuit, it is Nanuk and the six dogs chasing him.

Spider

Spiders may be small, but they have strong medicine. On the positive side, the spider represents skill and intelligence for the Blackfoot, and patience and endurance to the Ojibwa. A few people believed that the spider created the world by weaving it from her web. So positive spider medicine is often linked with females.

To many Plains people, such as the Dakota, Lakota, Nakoda and others, the spider is a trickster, sometimes named Iktomi. For the most part, Iktomi behaves in silly, inappropriate ways that get her in trouble.

Despite the mixed medicine of spiders from various cultures, most Native peoples believe that killing a spider is bad luck.

Although some people still call them bugs, spiders are not insects. They are arachnids. All but one species of spiders are predators. They mostly eat insects, but larger spiders have been known to prey on small birds and lizards.

If you follow the spider, you are patient. You can wait for a long periods for the proper moment. When that moment arrives, you strike instantly to achieve your goal. You are also a great builder who can connect "webs" between distant places and people, including connections with the spirit world.

Another reason why spiders are considered strong medicine is because of the creation and spread of one of the most identifiable and widespread symbols of North American Aboriginal Peoples: the dreamcatcher.

Many cultures believe that dreams come to people from the spirit world, rather than from the person's mind. The dreamcatcher helps to filter dreams so that bad dreams and nightmares get confused and become trapped in the web of the dreamcatcher. Good dreams are able to find their way through the web and into the mind of the sleeping person.

Dreamcatcher Legend (Anishinaabe)

One day long ago, Asibikaasi, the Anishinaabe grandmother spider, was spinning a web near the sleeping space of Nokomis, the grandmother.

Every day, Nokomis woke up seeing the light from the rising sun captured in the beautiful web. She spent many hours watching the spider build its web bigger and bigger.

After four days, the web was finished. But then one of Nokomis' grandsons came into her lodge and saw the spider web. He wanted to protect his grandmother so he picked up a rock, ready to destroy the web and kill Asibikaasi.

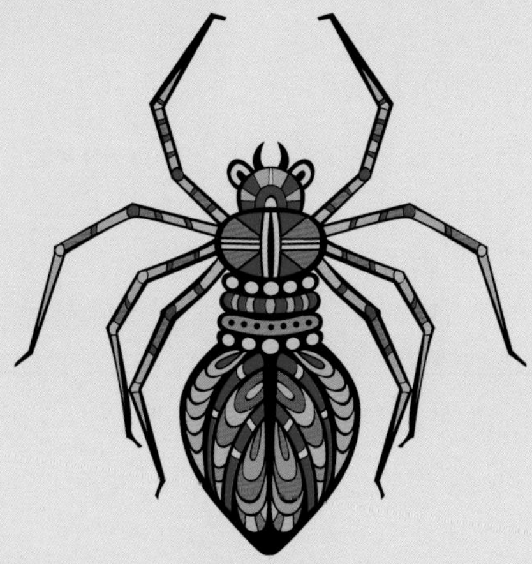

"Don't disturb Asibikaasi," the old woman whispered to the young boy. "And don't destroy the web."

"Why not, Nokomis?" the boy asked. "Why do you protect this spider?"

"Because Asibikaasi spent a long time building a beautiful home," replied Nokomis. "When the sun rises in the morning, I see the light captured by it, and it is wonderful.

And Asibikaasi protects me by catching and eating all the insects that would fly in and bite me. You should never destroy a web."

The boy nodded and left his grandmother, vowing that he would never destroy a spider web or kill a spider on purpose.

Later that night, Asibikaasi came to the grandmother in her dreams. She thanked the old woman for saving her life and her web.

"You have admired my work, and you have saved my life," said Asibikaasi. "In return, I will give you a gift."

Asibikaasi started spinning a web.

"Watch and learn," she said. "Bad dreams will be caught in the web and trapped. The good dreams will be able to fit through the small hole."

The next day, Asibikaasi left the grandmother's place, but left her web, the first dreamcatcher. Because of the dream, Nokomis knew how to make more, so she made one for her grandson and for all the other children. And she taught the people how to make dreamcatchers until everyone had one.

Wolf

Throughout history, the wolf has been one of the most feared animals. Scorned for centuries, they were hunted almost to extinction in Europe, and when the new-comers came to North America after 1492, they did the same to wolves here.

Native peoples held different views about the wolf than Europeans. The wolf was not an animal to be feared. It was respected and honored by almost every Native culture in North America. Like the bear, the wolf is thought to be like family to many Native peoples. It is called brother or cousin to humans.

Wolves are closer to humans than even bears. While bears are solitary creatures, wolves are social animals. They live in packs, most related to each other. They hunt together, working as an organized team to bring down their prey, in much the same way Native groups hunted together.

Although they are skilled hunters, they rarely attack animals that can defend themselves or get away quickly. Wolf medicine is closely associated with loyalty, strength, courage and, not surprisingly, success at hunting. Wolf clans are one of the most common of all Native clans. Many Native cultures believe the wolf taught humans how to live, hunt and raise families in a community. Its animal spirit is considered a wise teacher. Those born under the wolf sign or who belong to a wolf clan have this trait as part of their spirit.

The wolf symbolizes importance of family, protection of others and skill at communicating. Those whose spirit animal is the wolf possess many of these qualities. The wolf is deeply connected to the moon and avoids confrontation. However, if attacked, the wolf will fight back.

People who have the wolf as a spirit animal or totem feel uncomfortable with those who cannot freely communicate their feelings. If someone speaks over others too much, then a wolf can become impatient with that person.

If you encounter a wolf in the physical world, in a dream or during mediation or a spirit journey, it may mean it is time for you to become a teacher, either to yourself or someone else. Trust your instincts or your inner voice instead of the voices of others or those who claim to be teachers or guides.

Wolf and Lucky Man (Sahnish)

In the beginning was sky and water. In the sky there was Nesaru, the sky spirit, and Wolf and Lucky Man. Below the sky was a watery ocean. Two small ducks swam on the ocean making small, yet eternal, ripples.

Believing there could be more to the world than just the sky and the water, Wolf and Lucky Man asked the ducks to dive down and find mud. The ducks did as they were asked.

Wolf took half the mud and built a vast prairie for creatures like him, creatures who liked to hunt. Lucky Man built hills and valleys where the people could live and hunt.

Lastly, Wolf and Lucky Man pushed up the mud to create the banks of a river to divide their territories. Today, you can still see that river. It is the Missouri River.

And so the world was ready for life.

Wolf and Lucky Man knew that the smaller creatures would come first, and from them they would create the larger animals. So they went into the earth to find two spiders.

And so the spiders gave birth to the first creatures, eight-legged creatures like themselves. Over time, more creatures were born, those with six legs, then those with four legs, and finally, those with two, the People.

Beaver

No other animal, except humans, changes their landscape as the beaver does. They design and build dams out of trees, branches and mud. Their actions create large lakes, and in the middle of the lakes beavers build their lodges, homes for their families. What was once a simple stream through a thick forest is transformed into a diverse ecosystem with a wide variety of animals such as deer, moose, fish, wolves and insects.

Because beavers can change the landscape, many Native peoples, from the Chippewa, the Creek, the Huron, Mohawk, Tlingit, Kwakiutl and others, have beaver clans. Beavers represent handwork and building skills. People with the beaver as a spirit guide or totem are always busy. But they never take on more than they can handle. They just do the work that needs to be done.

Because beavers spend so much time in the water, people who follow the beaver love the water. In many cultures, water is connected to the spirit world so beavers are seen as good travelers in that realm. However, beavers cannot stay in that world forever. They must come up for air. Beavers can also be stubborn and sometimes work too hard without taking time to enjoy what they have built.

If you dream of a beaver or of a spirit that reminds you of a beaver, it may indicate that you have a project that needs to be done, and your only solution is to get it done. The vision of a beaver also means you have strong desire to fulfill your visions. If you work hard, you will succeed.

Finally, because beavers are great builders, they are seen as key characters in many creation myths.

Wisakedjak and the Great Beaver (Cree)

(Also spelled Wesakecha or Wisagatcak)

Not long after creating the world, Wisakedjak decided he wanted to capture the Great Beaver. So Wisakedjak built a giant dam across the river where the Great Beaver had its lodge.

"When the Great Beaver comes out," the trickster Wisakedjak said to himself, "I will attack him with a spear."

But the Great Beaver had strong magic. Just as Wisakedjak was about to throw the spear, the Great Beaver cast a spell that caused a muskrat to bite the trickster on his behind. Screaming in pain and surprise, Wisakedjak missed his target, and the Great Beaver survived. Even so, the Great Beaver vowed revenge.

Over several days, the Great Beaver and all the little beavers built so many dams that the world began to flood. Wisakedjak destroyed the dam he had built, but nothing would stop the water from rising. Before the entire world flooded, Wisakedjak built a raft out of the bits of wood from his dam and invited as many animals as possible onto the raft.

For two weeks, the water rose. The muskrat swam away to find land but even though the muskrat was a skilled swimmer, he drowned. The raven flew around the entire world but didn't find a single piece of land.

Because of all the moisture in the air, moss grew on Wisakedjak's raft. He gave the moss to the wolf and told him to run around the raft. The wolf did so, and using his own magic, Wisakedjak caused the moss to expand until the earth was rebuilt.

Today, water still springs out from the earth, from the holes in the original raft.

Duck

The duck is a funny-looking animal with a round body, an elongated neck and a flat bill. They may be ungainly on the land, waddling about on floppy webbed feet, but they are incredible swimmers. And amazing fliers. Ducks migrate thousands of miles each year between their winter and summer homes.

Because ducks are prey for foxes, wolves and other animals as well as humans, they are not seen as a major spirit animal. In much of Native folklore, ducks are seen as gullible creatures, continually conned and fooled by tricksters such as the coyote, wolverine and fox.

If you are of a duck clan or follow the duck as your spirit animal, you prefer to stay around your home, your "nest," to keep it safe. You are generous, have a big heart and love to be around others, especially those who have the same personality and outlook on life. Ducks are also resilient.

If the duck is your spirit animal, you love the water and can swim effortlessly. This skill allows you to build a stronger emotional balance that you can access during times of great hardship.

If a duck shows up in your life either through dreams or if you encounter the bird in real life, you are reaching a time of physicality, emotion or creativity. You should not deny yourself emotional and physical comfort. Finally, if you follow the duck animal spirit, you understand that life shouldn't be viewed so seriously. A duck knows that is wonderful to play and laugh, especially at oneself.

Shingebiss and Spirit of the North (Anishinaabe)

Shingebiss was a resourceful duck that lived in a lodge by a lake. She spent her days swimming in the lake and catching fish. One cold winter, Shingebiss stayed behind while the other ducks flew south for the winter.

At that time, the Anishinaabe also left the area for the winter because it was too cold, and there was not enough food for them to eat.

Not Shingebiss. When the lake froze, she cut a small hole in the ice to catch fish. She lit a fire in her lodge to keep warm.

Kabibona'kan, the Spirit of the North and the maker of winter, saw the duck living her life, unaffected by the cold and ice. Kabibona'kan was annoyed with the bird because the cold and the ice didn't bother her. He wanted to teach Shingebiss a lesson. So the Spirit of the North made the weather ten times colder and sent ten times more snow to freeze the duck out and force Shingebiss to fly south for the winter.

But Shingebiss was not affected by the colder weather. She continued to fish in her hole in the ice and live in her warm lodge with a fire.

Kabibona'kan decided that he would visit Shingebiss' lodge. He thought that his mere presence in the lodge would freeze the little duck out. When Kabibona'kan entered the lodge, Shingebiss just built up her fire more.

Suddenly Kabibona'kan began to notice his headdress of icicles was drooping. His clothes of ice and snow were becoming soggy and full of holes. Drops of water ran down his face. At first he thought he was crying, but he knew he didn't cry. He realized that he was melting, and if he didn't leave the lodge, he would melt to nothing.

The Spirit of the North figured that Shingebiss had powerful medicine and decided to leave her alone. He left the lodge and gave up trying to freeze out Shingebiss.

In the spring, the ducks returned and were surprised to find Shingebiss alive.

Although the ducks still head south for the winter, the Anishinaabe no longer do. Shingebiss taught them all the ways to stay warm and to find food in the winter.

Muskrat

Of all the spirit animals, the muskrat is probably the most underrated. Yet the muskrat is an important animal to many Native cultures. Almost every nation–Anishinaabe , Haudenosaunee (Iroquois Six Nations), Cree, Odawa, Potawatomi, Algonquin, Abenaki, Blackfoot—that lives or has lived in the habitat of the muskrat sees this small beaver-like mammal as a major spirit animal.

Like beavers, muskrats are nocturnal animals and spend much of their time swimming in water. Depending on the area where they live, muskrats live in dome-shaped lodges built out of sticks and mud or in burrows dug into the banks of rivers. Muskrats need a layer of snow over their lodges to stay warm, so many Native societies watch muskrats to predict winter snowfall.

If muskrats start building big lodges early, it is a sign of a mild winter with little snow. But if muskrats start building small lodges later in the year, after the frost comes, it means a harsh winter with lots of snow.

Many Native groups, including the Nimpuk people of New England, built their homes in the shape of a dome, a design borrowed from the muskrat. Because they can build their own homes, as well as predict the type of winter that will come, muskrats are seen as wise creatures.

If the muskrat is your animal spirit or you are part of a muskrat clan, you are well organized. You have a strong desire to live near or along a large body of water. Not surprisingly, you are a great swimmer and enjoy many kinds of water sports.

If a muskrat appears in your dreams, during meditation or a spiritual journey, it can mean that your life is getting too busy and noisy. It is time to clean up the clutter, be it physical or emotional. But never dismiss the muskrat because it is small. According to many Native myths, the muskrat was key in the creation of the world.

Creation of Turtle Island (Anishinaabe)

Long ago, after the world was created, the first people of the Earth began to stray from their harmonious ways. Brother turned against brother. People began to fight. Since harmony and respect for all living things was no longer on the Earth, Kitchi-Manitou (the Creator) decided to flood the world to purify it.

The Mush-ko-be-wun, the Great Flood, destroyed the people, their homes and many of the animals as well. Only Nanaboozhoo (a trickster figure and Anishinaabe cultural hero) managed to survive, along with a few animals.

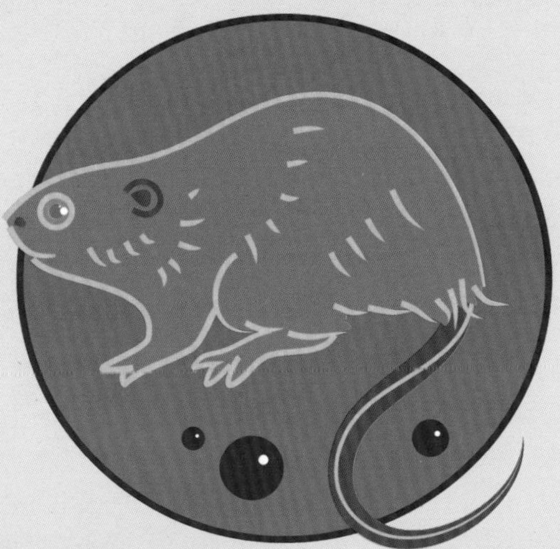

Nanaboozhoo clung to a huge log and searched for land. He could find none. He let the surviving animals take turns sitting on the log to rest.

After some time, Nanaboozhoo said, "I am going to swim to the bottom of this water to find some dirt of the old earth. With the dirt, I will create a new land for us to live on.

So Nanaboozhoo dove into the water. He was gone a long time. When he finally surfaced, he told the animals that the water was too deep for him.

"I can dive under the water for a long time," said Mahng, the loon. The loon dove and was also gone for a long time. The loon couldn't get to the bottom either. Neither could the grebe, the mink or the turtle.

Finally, the muskrat spoke in a small voice. "I can reach the bottom."

Some of the animals laughed. If they who were great swimmers couldn't reach the bottom, how could such a small creature?

Nanaboozhoo silenced the laughter. "If the muskrat wants to try, he can."

So the muskrat dove into the water. He was gone much longer than any of the other animals. Finally, the muskrat surfaced, but he had drowned. While the animals cried in grief, Nanaboozhoo saw a tiny bit of earth in muskrat's paw. It was enough for Nanaboozhoo to build the world again.

Orca

The orca (also called killer whale) is a powerful spirit animal, especially to the Pacific Coast peoples. Orcas were food for many coastal cultures and highly respected animals as the buffalo were to the Great Plains nations.

Unlike the buffalo, orcas are great hunters. They are called the sea wolves because they hunt in packs.

Orcas are in the dolphin family, so they are mammals. They are the fastest swimming mammals in the ocean with a maximum speed of 35 miles (56 kilometers) per hour. But orcas must surface every so often to breathe.

These animals are highly social. They live in tight-knit family groups called pods. Only elephants and higher primates such as apes and humans have more complex societies. Orca pods are always matriarchal. The animals live with their mothers for their entire lives. No animal strays from the group for more than a few hours at a time.

The orca's connection with the Pacific Coast peoples is likely because of their social behavior, their great ability to hunt and that these animals breathe air.

Overall, the orca is a positive animal spirit. Its appearance shows that your good friends and close family will help you reach your goals if you call on them. Having an experience with an orca may be a sign for you to call on that help.

Orcas are considered guardians of the earth with great medicine for healing. If you are of the orca clan or follow the orca as a spirit animal, you will sense that you must protect the earth and help heal others, whether in body, mind or spirit.

Orca medicine is strong, but it will not overpower you as some spirit animals do. The orca is a guardian, a social animal spirit that wishes to work with you to help you find your way.

Natsilane the Carver (Tlingit)

Long ago there lived a skilled hunter and wood carver named Natsilane. He married a chief's daughter from a nearby island and moved there to live with her family. At first he was accepted into the new clan and received great honor for his hunting and carving talents. But his new brothers-in-law were jealous of the hunter and decided to kill him.

During a seal hunt one day, Natsilane jumped out of the canoe to catch a sea lion. It escaped. When he tried to get back into the canoe, his brothers-in-law paddled away. They left him on a rocky island with no food or water. He waited for rescue, but no one came.

The next day, the hunter awoke to someone calling his name. It was a huge sea lion that looked like a man.

"My son was injured by a human spear, and we cannot get it out to save him," the sea lion said. "Can you help us?"

Natsilane said he would try. The sea lion asked Natsilane to follow him to the bottom of the ocean. Natsilane wasn't sure if he could survive under the water. But he thought he would probably die on the rock island anyway, so he followed the sea lion. The sea lion took him to the chief's house.

In the house lay the injured sea lion. Natsilane removed the spear and saved the sea lion's life. In thanks for saving his son, the chief of the sea lions gifted Natsilane with magic to improve his carving skills. The sea lion took him back to his village where he was reunited with his wife. He told her what had happened with her brothers.

The next day, Natsilane went into the woods with his carving tools. He carved a huge black fish out of some special spruce. When he put the carving in the water, it became many large, black fish that came to life.

Because he was their creator, the black fish asked him what they could do for him. Natsilane told them to find his brothers-in-law and sink their canoe so they would drown. The fish did as they were told, but the brothers survived. They told the others in the village about the great black fish.

Natsilane knew he should not have tried to kill his sister's brothers. He told the black fish to never harm humans again. They listened to him.

Every so often, the black fish, now called orcas, show respect to Natsilane by leaving a freshly killed seal or other fish near the shore for the people to eat.

Salmon

Salmon are important animals to the Pacific West Coast people. For them and the peoples on the Atlantic Coast, salmon was a primary food source.

Salmon are migratory creatures. They are born in fresh water and migrate to the ocean where they live for many years. Finally, they swim upstream hundreds of miles to return to the river where they were born to lay their eggs. During their journey, they pass the lands of many Native peoples who fish the salmon for food.

Because of its cycle of life, the salmon is a key species for the Pacific Northwest and Alaska. These fish are a food source for humans, birds and other animals, such as otters, bears and orcas. Salmon even impact the forests. Nearly half of the salmon that bears catch are left uneaten on the forest floor to decompose. As a result, nearly one-quarter of the nitrogen, a nutrient needed for plant life, comes from salmon that bears leave behind.

Salmon are known for finding their way back to their spawning grounds after many years in the ocean. Those who follow the salmon as a spirit animal are excellent at finding their way. They also know what they want and how to achieve it. They finish what they start no matter the obstacles.

If you encounter a salmon, it could mean it is time to trust your gut and allow it to guide you to your destination. You may face many challenges in the future, but you will eventually find your way.

The Four Brothers (Squamish)

A long time ago, when humans and animals spoke the same language, there were four brothers who liked to help the people.

One day, the brothers visited the Squamish people.

"Can you bring the salmon to our village?" asked the chief. "We are often short of food. We know that the salmon are good, but they never come to our shores."

"We will talk to the salmon people and ask them," said the eldest brother.

The four brothers asked the sun where to look for the salmon. When they had an answer, they went back to the Squamish.

"Get your canoes and prepare for a long journey," said the eldest brother. "At sunrise, we will leave to visit the salmon."

The next morning they started out and paddled for many days. Finally, they came to an island with what seemed to be a village near the shore. Smoke of all colors rose up into the clouds.

"This looks like what we are searching for," said the brothers.

The paddlers landed their canoes on the broad, smooth beach. The Squamish people walked toward the village. The four brothers carried some medicine with them. They gave the medicine to Spring Salmon, the chief of the village. He was friendly.

The time came to welcome the strangers with a feast. The chief ordered others to go to a salmon trap and bring back the four fish they would find there. He told them to clean and roast the fish for their guests. When the salmon were cooked, the chief invited his guests to eat. The Squamish knew that they had finally found the salmon people.

"My friends are poor, and they often go hungry," said the eldest brother to the chief. "Will you visit them so they can eat.

"I will do as you ask, on one condition," said the salmon chief. "The people must throw all the bones back into the water as we have done. If you do this and are careful with the bones, my people can return home to us, after they visit and feed you. Do you promise?"

The Squamish and the four brothers all promised.

Ever since that time, the salmon have visited the Squamish. The people are always careful to return the bones to the sea.

Turtle

Turtles, especially North American species, are small reptiles. They are shy and not known as great hunters. They may live for more than 100 years, but they live quietly. Even though they are air-breathing animals, most of their time is spent underwater.

Because of the turtle's quiet nature, one may think it is not a strong spirit animal. But turtles have a special place in the lives of many Indigenous Peoples.

From Cree to Blackfoot, and Iroquois to Lenape and many other cultures, the turtle is a major character in creation stories. These stories usually begin after a great flood and after the Creator became angry with the people of the world. Because the turtle can swim, it does not die in the flood. Its hard shell and broad back becomes a raft for the animals that survived the flood.

These stories often include another character with magical powers—a trickster or a cultural hero. Using dirt taken from the sea floor, the trickster/hero rebuilds the earth on

the back of the turtle. That is why for many Native peoples, North America is called Turtle Island.

Because many believe the world was built on the back of a turtle, this animal reflects respect for Mother Earth. The turtle represents peace with Mother Earth and all its inhabitants.

If you follow the turtle as a spirit animal, you have a deep connection with Mother Earth. You may have hidden strength not noticed by others, but it is there. Also, the turtle is connected to healing and protection.

If you follow the turtle spirit animal, you move at your own pace, not ignorant of others and their needs, but with focus. Most people will see that and will not try to rush you. They know you are on task and always deliver.

The turtle lives its own life, quietly doing what it needs to do, without feeling pressure to move faster. The turtle is one of the most honored creatures, not just by Aboriginal peoples but also by other cultures. The Chinese and Hindu also see the world being carried on its strong back.

Always remember, you live on Turtle Island.

The Legend of the Turtle Shell (Anishinaabe)

One day Nanaboozhoo (the Anishinaabe cultural hero) awoke cranky and hungry. So he went to the village to find something to eat. He came upon some men cooking fish. He asked for some fish, and the men gave him some. It was hot. When he grabbed the fish, it burnt his hand. He ran to the lake to put his hand in the water to cool it off. Because he was still groggy, Nanaboozhoo tripped on a rock. He fell on Mishekae, a turtle. Back then Mishekae did not have a shell. She was only made of soft skin and bone.

Mishekae screamed in pain, saying, "Nanaboozhoo, watch where you are going!"

Nanaboozhoo was ashamed that he had hurt the turtle. She was a nice creature and didn't bother anyone.

He apologized then wondered, *What can I do to make it up to her?*

Nanaboozhoo thought for a while. Then he saw two large shells on the shore. He put the shells together, picked up Mishekae and put her in between them.

"There you go. Now no one will ever hurt you again," he said. "And when danger comes, you can pull in your legs and your head to protect yourself."

Mishekae thought the shells were wonderful. She practiced sticking her feet, her head and her tail out of the shells. Nanaboozhoo watched and realized something important.

"The shell is round like the Earth. Because you have four legs, each one will represent north, south, east and west," Nanaboozhoo said. "The people will see you, and you will give them messages. When you draw your legs in, they will know that danger is near, and all direction is lost. Your tail will show where they have been, and your head will show them where they should go.

"You will also be able to live in the water as well as on the land because you carry your house on your back."

Mishekae loved her new shell and thanked Nanaboozhoo for his wisdom. She pushed herself along the shore and disappeared into the water. Because Nanaboozhoo had shown her kindness after hurting her, the people see Mishekae as a special animal.

About the Author

Photo by Maki Blazevski.

Award-winning author Wayne Arthurson is a freelance writer of Cree descent. He has written professionally for over 20 years and has worked full time as a journalist, editor, communications officer and an advertising copywriter. He has more than 100 articles, five history books and three novels already published, including the award-winning *Fall From Grace.* He is also the author of an expanded version of *Spirit Animals: The Wisdom of Nature, In the Shadow of Our Ancestors* and *Ghost Detective* (under the pen name Zachary Muswagon) for Eschia Books.

Spirit Animals

Meanings & Stories

Our Aboriginal Elders tell of a time when animals and humans could speak to each other. When humans became too greedy and killed more animals than they needed for food, the Creator changed that relationship to protect the animals. So the Creator made a Spirit Animal to represent each one and granted them gifts they could give to people.

Spirit Animals teach, heal and inspire. Turtle carries North America on its back and symbolizes peace and balance. Bear is called "Grandfather" for its strength, leadership, confidence and courage. Coyote gifted us with fire and knowledge of herbs and food. Wolf taught us to hunt and form communities.

This book is a guide, and the meanings of the Spirit Animals featured here are only one interpretation. If you see these Spirit Animals or Totems reflected in your own life, you have received their gift.

$9.99

Printed in China